D1014546

Claudia "Lady Bird" Johnson

ENVIRONMENTAL PROTECTOR

BY TYLER OMOTH

Published by The Child's World®
1980 Lookout Drive • Mankato, MN 56003-1705
800-599-READ • www.childsworld.com

Photographs ©: Hulton Archive/Archive Photos/Getty Images, cover, 1; Lyndon Baines Johnson Presidential Library and Museum photo by Robert Knudsen, 5; Schulmann-Sachs/picture-alliance/dpa/Newscom, 6; Everett Collection/Newscom, 8, 12, 14, 18; Cecil Stoughton/KRT/Newscom, 10; Keystone Pictures USA/Alamy, 16; Rodger Mallison/KRT/Newscom, 20

ISBN 9781503823952
LCCN 2017944734

Printed in the United States of America
PA02362

ABOUT THE AUTHOR

Tyler Omoth has written more than 30 books for kids, covering a wide variety of topics. He has also published poetry and award-winning short stories. He loves sports and new adventures. Tyler currently lives in sunny Brandon, Florida, with his wife, Mary.

TABLE OF
CONTENTS

FAST FACTS

Full Name

- Claudia Alta "Lady Bird" Taylor Johnson

Birthdate

- December 22, 1912, in Karnack, Texas

Husband

- President Lyndon B. Johnson

Children

- Lynda and Luci

Years in White House

- 1963–1969

Accomplishments

- Pushed for the Highway Beautification Act, which was designed to promote nature and the planting of wildflowers along major highways and near cities.

- Promoted civil rights during her famous **whistle-stop tour** in 1964.

- Helped launch the Head Start Program, which has helped more than 30 million children in **poverty**.

- Supported the "War on Poverty" in the United States.

Chapter 1

A DETERMINED WOMAN

It was 1964, and Claudia "Lady Bird" Johnson sat on the edge of her seat. Her husband, President Lyndon B. Johnson, was giving his annual "State of the Union" address. "This administration, today, here and now, declares unconditional war on poverty in America," he said.[1] Part of his plan to eliminate poverty was to improve education for the poor. Lady Bird clapped along with the hundreds of people in attendance. She knew that this was a cause she could champion. She would be remembered as the First Lady who fought against poverty and lack of education for children in the United States.

◀ Lady Bird was very active as First Lady. She supported many different causes.

▲ Lady Bird first hated the nickname that her nurse, Alice, gave her. Later, she grew to love it.

As a child, Lady Bird did not struggle with poverty. Instead, she had a family and a nurse who took care of her. Her nurse's name was Alice Tittle.

One day, two-year-old Claudia was playing on the lawn in a new dress. Alice looked at her and said, "My, isn't she just as pretty as a lady bird!"[2] From that day forward everyone called her Lady Bird.

Lady Bird was a determined young woman. She planned to become a journalist. But instead, she married a young politician named Lyndon Johnson. She dedicated herself to managing his campaigns, home affairs, and finances. In 1942, Lady Bird purchased a radio station. Later, she bought a TV station. She managed both and built a sizable fortune.

While Lady Bird managed the businesses, Lyndon pursued his political career. In 1960, his big break came. Presidential hopeful John F. Kennedy asked Lyndon to be his vice presidential candidate. The pair won the election. In 1961, Lyndon was sworn in as vice president of the United States of America. For Lady Bird, this meant that she'd have an opportunity to take her passions to the national stage.

Chapter 2

BEAUTIFYING AMERICA

It was a beautiful, sunny day in Dallas, Texas, on November 22, 1963. Lady Bird and her husband rode in a convertible going slowly through the city. They were on a campaign tour with President John F. Kennedy. As they drove through Dallas, people lined the streets and waved. The Johnsons waved back to them from their car. They were just two cars behind the president in the **motorcade**. Suddenly, the sound of gunshots rang out. Someone had targeted John F. Kennedy. He was **assassinated**. Just two hours later, Lady Bird was standing next to her husband on an airplane.

◀ **Lady Bird (left) stood by her husband as he was suddenly sworn in as the 36th president of the United States.**

▲ Lyndon signed the bill for the Highway Beautification Act on October 22, 1965.

Lyndon was sworn in as president of the United States. Lady Bird could not believe that she was suddenly the First Lady.

In 1964, as she traveled the country with Lyndon, Lady Bird noticed that cities were getting bigger.

There were more highways than ever. Nature was getting pushed out in the name of progress. As First Lady, she was determined to use her position to make a difference.

So Lady Bird created the First Lady's Committee for a More Beautiful Capital. She also promoted **legislation** called the Highway Beautification Act of 1965. She was determined to do whatever she could to keep her country's landscape beautiful and healthy. Every day as she drove along the highways of Washington, DC, she could see that her plan was working.

"A beautification in my mind is far more than a matter of cosmetics. To me, it describes the whole effort to bring the natural world and the manmade world to harmony. To bring order, usefulness, delight to our whole environment. And that of course only begins with trees and flowers and landscaping."[3]

– Lady Bird Johnson

Chapter 3

CIVIL RIGHTS WHISTLE-STOP TOUR

Lady Bird looked out of the train window as the engine and its cars click-clacked to a stop. It was the fall of 1964, and the train was pulling into Richmond, Virginia. She was traveling across the Southern states on a whistle-stop tour, promoting the Civil Rights Act. Lyndon had recently signed the act into a law. As the train pulled up to the station, Lady Bird saw a large crowd. Many of them were cheering and waving. But in the back, one man held up a large sign that said, "Fly away, Lady Bird!" Not everyone wanted to hear what she had to say.

Lady Bird thought about how good the Civil Rights Act was. It put an end to **segregation** in public places.

◀ Lady Bird (center) visited eight Southern states in four days on her train tour.

▲ Lady Bird later wrote a book about her experience as First Lady called *A White House Diary.*

The act made it illegal for employers to **discriminate** based on race, religion, gender, or national origin. Lady Bird had grown up in the South. She knew that not everyone was in favor of the law. She was determined to change their minds.

Lady Bird continued on her tour. She watched the countryside go by her train window for four days, covering 1,628 total miles (2,620 km). She wished her husband could be along with her. But he was busy in Washington, DC. This tour was something she had to do on her own. It was something no First Lady had ever done before.

"I knew the Civil Rights Act was right and I didn't mind saying so."[5]

– Lady Bird Johnson

When the tour ended, Lady Bird picked up a newspaper. Journalist Max Freedman had covered her tour. He wrote a story about it. In it he said, "Perhaps this marks the **emergence** of women as central figures in a national contest instead of being on the edges of a campaign."[4]

Chapter 4

GIVING KIDS A HEAD START

A small group of children sat in their chairs, looking up at Lady Bird. She sat in a small chair in their classroom in Washington, DC, wearing a bright-yellow dress. She was reading to them from one of their favorite books. The class was part of a program called Head Start. This program aimed to help young people in poor neighborhoods. Through the program they would receive education, nutrition, and health services. Lady Bird wanted to help those who needed it most.

Lady Bird loved the idea from the beginning. But she was not certain that the public would be as enthusiastic. "The Head Start idea has such hope and challenge. . . .

◀ Lady Bird's first school visit as part of the Head Start program was to Kemper School in Washington, DC.

▲ Lady Bird continued to work in politics, including helping plan the Lyndon Baines Johnson Library and Museum.

Maybe I could help focus public attention in a favorable way on some aspects of Lyndon's poverty program," she said.[6]

With the help of Lady Bird, the Head Start program was launched. The program still runs today in every state. Head Start has helped more than 30 million children in poverty.

As First Lady, Lady Bird knew that she had the power to help a new program such as Head Start. She did everything she could to help it thrive. Lady Bird worked with the program not just as First Lady, but throughout her life. The program was successful and still operates today. After her death in 2007, Lady Bird Johnson was named an **honorary** chairwoman of Head Start.

THINK ABOUT IT

- Lady Bird Johnson used her position as First Lady to promote causes that she believed in. If you had that kind of power, what causes would you want to help?
- The Highway Beautification Act was put in place to keep nature beautiful and healthy as cities grew bigger. Do you think we do enough today to promote nature?
- The Civil Rights Act of 1964 eliminated segregation and promoted equal hiring practices. How do you think the United States is different today because of this law?

GLOSSARY

assassinated (uh-SAS-uh-nay-ted): Assassinated is when an important person is killed for political or religious reasons. Lady Bird was there on the day that John F. Kennedy was assassinated.

discriminate (dis-KRIM-i-nate): To discriminate is to treat people unfairly based on their race or gender. Lady Bird knew that to discriminate against others was wrong.

emergence (i-MURJ-ens): The emergence of something means it has come into view. Lady Bird's nationwide tour marked the emergence of First Ladies as central figures in a campaign.

honorary (AH-nuh-rayr-ee): An honorary title or gift is given to honor someone. Lady Bird was named honorary chairwomen of the Head Start program.

legislation (lej-is-LAY-shun): Legislation is another term for a law passed by the government. Lady Bird promoted the legislation for the Highway Beautification Act.

motorcade (MOH-tur-kade): A motorcade is a procession of vehicles that includes an important person or persons. Lady Bird was a part of the motorcade when John F. Kennedy was killed.

poverty (PAH-vur-tee): To be in poverty is to be very poor. Lady Bird supported the War on Poverty.

segregation (seg-ri-GAY-shun): Segregation is a separation of racial groups in a country or community that is enforced by law. Lady Bird wanted to help end segregation.

whistle-stop tour (WIS-ul STAHP TOOR): A whistle-stop tour is a political campaign tour that stops at several small towns or cities. Lady Bird Johnson went on a four-day whistle-stop tour through the South.

SOURCE NOTES

1. Robert Rector and Rachel Sheffield. "War on Poverty after 50 Years." *Heritage.org*. The Heritage Foundation, 14 Sept. 2014. Web. 27 June 2017.

2. "Lady Bird Johnson: The Early Years." *PBS.org*. Public Broadcasting Service, 2001. Web. 27 June 2017.

3. "Lady Bird Johnson." *Biography.org*. A&E Television Networks, 27 Apr. 2017. Web. 27 June 2017.

4. "Lady Bird Johnson: At the Epicenter." *PBS.org*. Public Broadcasting Service, 2001. Web. 27 June 2017.

5. Ibid.

6. Katherine A. S. Sibley. *A Companion to First Ladies*. Hoboken, NJ: John Wiley & Sons, 2016. Print. 525.

TO LEARN MORE

Books

Krull, Kathleen. *A Kids' Guide to America's First Ladies*. New York, NY: HarperCollins, 2017.

Roberts, Cokie. *Founding Mothers: Remembering the Ladies*. New York, NY: HarperCollins, 2014.

Yasuda, Anita. *Lady Bird Johnson*. New York, NY: Weigl, 2011.

Web Sites

Visit our Web site for links about Lady Bird Johnson:

childsworld.com/links

Note to Parents, Teachers, and Librarians: We routinely verify our Web links to make sure they are safe and active sites. So encourage your readers to check them out!

INDEX